F IS FOR FLAG

 By Wendy Cheyette Lewison
Illustrated by Barbara Duke

Grosset & Dunlap
An Imprint of Penguin Group (USA), Inc.

Library of Congress Cataloging-in-Publication Data
Lewison, Wendy Cheyette.
F is for flag / by Wendy Cheyette Lewison ; illustrated by Barbara Duke.
p. cm.
Summary: Celebrates the origin, symbolism, and power of the banner that represents the United States of America. 1. Flags—United States—Juvenile literature.
[1. Flags—United States.] I. Duke, Barbara (Barbara J.) ill. II. Title.
CR113.L57   2002
929.9'2'0973—dc21   2002003913
ISBN 978-0-448-42838-3   H I J

F is for "flag." Our flag.
The American flag.

See it waving in the wind,
just like a hand waving hello.

Our flag is everywhere—
at the library and in the park, even on letters we send.
We see our flag near and far. At school ...

...and on ships at sea.

We see our flag—in happy times and sad times.
Our flag is so many places because we are proud of it.

It stands for our country, the United States of America.
And it stands for us, the people who live here.

Who are we?

We are all kinds of people—different in many ways.

But we live and work and play together.
We are like one great big family.
One country, one family, one flag for everybody.

The first American flag was made more than 200 years ago. That's when America became a country. Who made the first flag? No one really knows. One story says Betsy Ross made it after George Washington asked her to.

Snip, snip, snip! Betsy cut and sewed.
Soon the flag was finished.

The first flag looked different. It had 13 stars and 13 stripes. That's because there were only 13 states when the United States first became a country. Today our country is bigger.

We have 50 states now, and our flag has 50 bright stars, one for each state. But our flag still has 13 stripes to remember the first 13 states.

The colors of our flag are the same—
red, white and blue. Sometimes we even
call our flag the "Red, White, and Blue."
We've given our flag a nickname.
We have other nicknames for our flag, too—
"Stars and Stripes," "Old Glory," and
"Star-Spangled Banner."

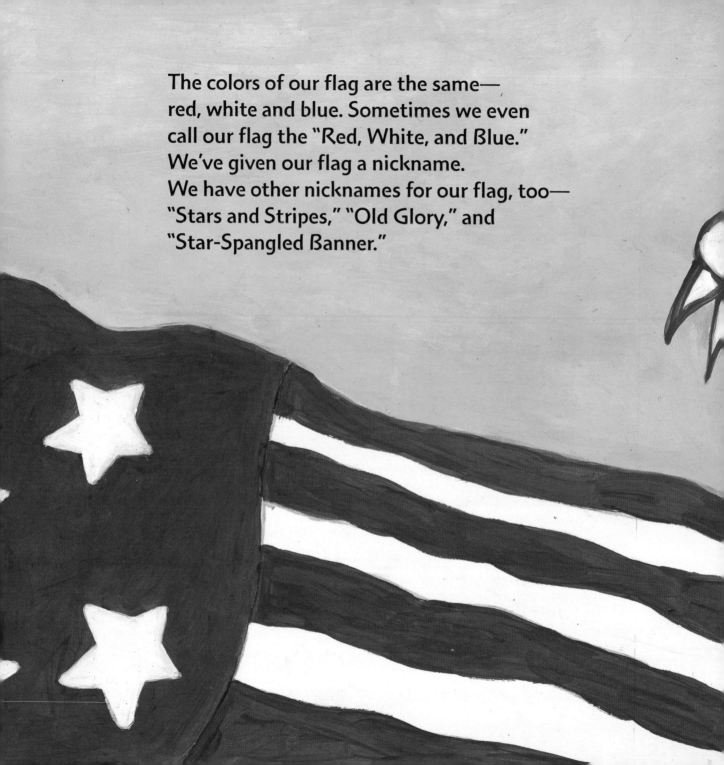

"The Star-Spangled Banner" is also
the name of our country's song.

It's a song all about our flag. Sometimes when we hear it, tears come to our eyes.

We are proud of our flag. We have songs about it.
We have nicknames for it. We have the Pledge of Allegiance, too.

The Pledge of Allegiance

I pledge Allegiance to the flag of the United States of America and to the republic for which it stands one nation under God indivisible with liberty and justice for all.

The Pledge is a promise—a promise to be a good American, a promise to be a good friend to our flag. As we make this promise, we hold our hand over our heart. This shows that we mean what we say.

F is for "flag." Our flag.
F is for family and friends and freedom, too—
and everything special that our flag stands for.
F is also for Flag Day—June 14—our flag's birthday.
On Flag Day, big parades march down streets all over America.

Boom, boom, boom! go the drums.
Here comes the Red, White, and Blue!
Hooray for our flag—today...

...and every day!